ATTEMPTS AT TRUTH

DEANNA SYLVESTER

Copyright © 2019 by Deanna Sylvester

All rights reserved

Printed in the United States of America

Thank you for buying an authorized edition of this book and for not reproducing, scanning, or distributing any part of it in any form without written permission. You are supporting independent writers and artists by complying with these copyright laws.

Cover photos taken by the author.

ISBN 978-0-578-61484-7

to Me
for my 50th birthday

to Loren and Dad and Mom
for allowing me to grow up so freely

to Hailey
for giving me an unimagined purpose

and to Sabra
because, you are

Contents

I Write	1
Wind	3
Tease	5
Totem	7
Parenting	9
My Precious Child	11
Like the Ocean	13
Some Times	15
Her Hands	17
My Green	19
Let Go	21
Falling in Love	23
Symphony	25
My Only Prayer	26
Make Your Own Mosaic	29
True Love	31
Wavelengths	33
My Only Regrets	35
Mo_urning	37
Chance of Rain	39
Binary Stars	41

Bloom	43
Red-Tailed Haikus	45
Smell of Rain	47
Whole	49
Cowgirl	51
Impermanence	53
The Ultimate Gift	54
Longing	57
She Is the Desert	59
Leaving Town	61
Rain in the Desert	63
Angels	65
Accidental Meeting	67
The Perfect Evening	69
Shooting Star	71
Upper Hand	73
Seeds	75
Metamorphosis	77
Dream Me Home	79
Aging	81
Walk with Cardinal	83

Attempts at Truth

I Write

I close my eyes
feeling the breeze

the only way I will ever feel
this world

at times too much, throbbing
way too much

I write with my heart
sometimes nature
helps me start

I open my eyes
and through them I see

the only view I will ever have
of the world

at times too bright, painful
way too bright

I write what I see
sometimes nature
sometimes me

Wind

the wind
on my face

comes with dust
in my eye

irritating grit
burn

blink
blink

but, ah, the wind
on my face

I squint
and I smile

TEASE

Could have been Sharp-shinned,
could have been Cooper,
but she was indifferent
to my address of her.

Parked only for a moment
at the top of the pole,
she said, "thanks for the visit,
but breakfast's my goal."

She opened her wings
and with one nudge of breeze,
I swear, she winked at me
as she lifted. What a tease.

Totem

the hawk flies free
of limiting beliefs
balancing clear vision with sensitivity

up where optimism is accepted truth

with one wing in the heavens
and one dipped toward the earth
she delivers the messages of spirit

through ordinary experiences
if only I notice

Parenting

do your own sewing
do your own mending

wear bravely the sleeve
to which you've sewn your own heart

you never have to worry about the occasion,
you'll always be appropriately dressed

My Precious Child

No blood of mine runs through your veins
but when you're cut I bleed

No breath of mine has filled your chest
but seeing you I breathe

I did not bring you to this world
your genes I do not know

By fate you're here and I'm fulfilled
to simply watch you grow

My body knows no labor pains
my pain's deeper, more sublime

The beat in my heart bears your name
though you're no blood of mine

Like the Ocean

I could have stayed in the boat,
or just waded around in it.

But I jumped in,
unable to swim,
I learned what it feels like
to breathe underwater.

There's pain, then
bearable pain, then
paradise.

Like the ocean,
Love is always there.

And drowning
is the only option
to fully live.

Some Times

at times
I'm like the Quail
easily spooked
running everywhere
though I have wings

at times
I'm like the Cougar
relaxed, conserving
then attacking
when scared or hungry

at times
I'm like the Tree
sturdy, dependable,
confident
in any storm

and sometimes
I *am* the Quail
I *am* the Cougar
I *am* the Tree
I am, at once, all these things
I am me

Her Hands

the key of life is in her hands
on her hands

a map revealed in the cracks
worn and tired

unique beautiful lines
carved by laughter and tears
love and pain

by grace they came to be
by fate they came to me

in the perfect condition
to love again

My Green

there must be 100 shades of green
in my current view
facing west across the desert
each one a slight variation of the next

and I love them all, to be sure
but that one there, she takes my breath
surprising me
dazzling, delightful, delicious

others notice
but no one else really sees
that green
the only green for me

Let Go

fall
like water

without
a specific destination

just
keep falling

down
down

knowing
you will reach the ocean

Falling in Love

I wanted to write something beautiful
but I thought of your smile
and the words littered nonsense

I wanted to write something warm
but I thought of your touch
and the cold paper contrast stared

I wanted to write something sweet
but I thought of your lips
and the sentence whispered bitter

I wanted to write something, anything
but I thought of your spirit
and my pen fell silent wanting

You touch me in a place where
my thoughts can no longer come together
in a smooth flow

words hit the page in ridiculous
fashion so that you have to look
into my eyes to receive the meaning

Don't look away
I'm not finished flailing

Symphony

as the sunrise colors the sky
the rainbow appears in crescendo

sweet violet red harmonies
a symphony of pink and yellow

and the pulsing orange sun
continues its rhythmic hue

up, up
as the colors fade to blue

My Only Prayer

Your heart beats—
our hearts jump for joy.
My belly grows our baby boy.

I feel you move—
our world is moved.
Changed forever
by your gentle stirring
and moments of peace.

The worry, the excitement.
But now, the longing
for you as my breasts drip
a purpose unfulfilled onto my shirt.

Your lungs weren't ready,
and neither are mine,
surprised at the pain
of each forced inhalation.

I have no choice, just like you.

My heart beats—
though broken.
A delicate balance,
the tenderest flesh on the edge
of the sharpest instrument.
A small breeze could push me into it.

But the face of the tiniest,
beautiful boy holds me back.

I take the next painful breath
and blink the tears from my eyes.

I miss you.
I don't remember life without you.

My only prayer
to see you in heaven
and rock you to sleep for eternity.

Make Your Own Mosaic

I may be broken
but that doesn't mean
something's wrong with me

broken
may be
necessary

some of these pieces
don't go
together anyway

with patience, I can choose
more lovely
pieces along the way

until the colorful continuation

is a mosaic of my own creation

If you're struggling to hold your shit together, at least make sure it's your own shit—not something handed down to you through generations or by the well-meaning "helpers" of today.

In fact, being broken, breaking it all apart, may be the only way to identify yourself to yourself. And then you can pick up and hold together just those pieces that fit your own heart.

The load becomes lighter as you sift through the wreckage one by one. Plus, you have a much clearer view when you are standing on top of that mountain of crap that was never your shit anyway.

True Love

wildflowers always smile at the sun
no matter their location
or impending fate

the roll of the truck tire
the appetite of the mule deer
the misplaced heel of my boot

smiles last as long as they can
when they are looking at their one true love

Wavelengths

green leaves
red and yellow petals
blue water

all rejects of light

while the other
wavelengths
are absorbed

by the tree
by the flowers
by the stream

the rejected light
finds its way
to certain pupils

accepted

by open eyes
that see beauty
even in rejects

My Only Regrets

why did I waste that time,
that time we sat looking
at the waves crashing
and didn't grab your hand

why did I squander any,
every, second
I could have been
kissing your lips

why did any words fall
from my lips
in your direction
other than the truth,
"I adore you"

MO_U_RNING

this morning I'm comforted
by the sunrise
predictable
warm, radiant
a reminder of what I am inside

and the burning bush welcomes me
wiping the sleep from my eyes
with its pink and yellow glow
awakening, with each breath I remember
even in mourning the world says hello

Chance of Rain

The sun,
warm on my legs,
warm on my face,
teases me with the possibility,
"Go on, I dare you to feel wonderful."

I can see it in the distance.

It looks like her.

But, no, not today.

And the clouds cry with me.

Binary Stars

In the space between
I consider my plight
You consider yours

Experiencing our own spins
        our individual orbits

Some forces spin us apart
        the same forces bring us back

Where we accept each other
        ourselves just as we are

Forever linked across the illusion of space

Bloom

the sun rises over the same world
but nothing's the same

the new bud, soft and fragile,
lifts her head toward the light

she knows she's been here before

she knows that plenty others
don't make it

and still —

she knows it's the only way

it's full-bloom or nothing
for this tiny flower

Red-tailed Haikus

thank you miss red-tail
for visiting and talking
to me this morning

cheew cheew cheew cheew cheeeew
what mind does not comprehend
the heart understands

Smell of Rain

the sun on the Creosote
damp, oily
reminds me of rain

Eddie returns from
exploration
"what did you find out?" I ask

startled by the Curved Bill thrashing
I do not get an answer
he's off again

so much to find
on his own
not so much to share

I'm sure he knows the truth
but politely
keeps it to himself

so I wait
and rub the Creosote
between my fingers

I smell the rain
I listen to the Thrasher
what else could I do anyway

Whole

our feelings, desires,
courage and consciousness
wax and wane
just like the moon

what a relief
the entire moon
though sometimes hidden
is always there
complete in her wholeness

even in crescent
the moon is not lost or broken
patiently revealing herself anew
in perfect timing

as do we

Cowgirl

she speaks to the cows
I suppose because they speak to her
in the language of the wind

an ongoing conversation
of which I'm only aware
because of that distant stare

in her eyes

she often barely tolerates
the people noise, the dog bark
but then I catch a glimpse—the spark

in her eyes

she must be hearing
the cows again
in the language of the wind

Impermanence

waking from dreams
I realize
I'm here again

and there's the sun
behind the mountain
behind the clouds

it will always be there

it's the only thing that will

The Ultimate Gift

for years, big sister
grasped at every way she knew
to love and support
        the baby girl
        the wounded child
        the distant woman
        and the dying soul

and she succeeded
through all eyes but her own

no one should have to bear life and death that way

and she should not have had to witness it
desperate, longing, helpless
becoming
        the baby girl
        the wounded child
        the distant woman
        the dying soul herself

and she succeeded
through her very own eyes

but being that perfect, tragic, intimate witness
to the coming
and the going

        was the ultimate gift
        a sister could ever give

        the only thing
        she could have ever done

and she succeeded
through the eyes of her baby sister

Longing

While lenticular clouds hold their ground
and resolute Crow teases me,
a lone Dragonfly paints the wind.
Now two.
Now five.

They paint right through the longing.
And the Dandelion grows.
The Dandelion grows anyway!
"Why?" I ask. The wind
whispers, "until all wishes survive."

She Is the Desert

the desert calls to herself
whatever she needs

she stirs the sea
and the wind brings her rain

she stirs the heart
and love heals her pain

Leaving Town

Kneeling on the sidewalk in Judgment,
grasping at the fragments of my pride,
my gaze wanders up the leg of Acceptance,
confident and swift in her stride.

It's difficult to assemble the pieces.
I'm blinded by the naked glare.
Acceptance calls me to follow her,
but mine are scraped knee and blank stare.

My hands reach up to grab at her skirt.
My heart begs her to slow down.
Ah, my lips won't move, I can't cry out,
my betraying voice makes no sound.

She rounds the corner just out of sight.
In my dream she always travels alone.
But I can't stay forever on a sidewalk in Judgment.
Leaning back on my heels, I stand on my own.

Rain in the Desert

clouds hug the mountains
like absolute lovers

and the valley softens

her inhabitants
relax in the moist embrace

not one worries

not yet

it's inevitable anyway

so for now

they dance in the rain
as if there's only today

Angels

with my heart wide open
the angels appear
bringing me messages
only I can hear

compassion and patience
allow and just be
slowing down, sinking in
forgiveness is me

Accidental Meeting

oh, that smile
oh, that touch
what could I possibly say

breathe, just breathe
only love
love made it happen today

The Perfect Evening

bouncing whistles
of Western Screech
accelerating through the night

interrupted by the
Great Horned bark
longing for her lover

guwaay
guwaay

is it the silence
or the longing
or the sweet bouncing whistle
that calls me into the night?

yes

and yet —

it could simply be
the powerful summons
from the deep well
of her hazel eyes

Shooting Star

I stared at Orion
I tried not to blink
waiting
waiting for a burst of light
so brief, so brilliant

it takes patience
it takes trust
it takes a warm coat

I stood close to her
I tried not to think
waiting
waiting for a spark of love
so short, so sweet

it takes patience
it takes trust
it takes a warm heart

shooting stars don't often
come into view
but when you can catch one
it changes you

Upper Hand

you say I have the Upper Hand
and so I imagine
all the things my hands can do
with such an advantage

> help you up when you fall
> block the sun from your eyes
> wipe away your tears
>
> applaud your successes
> console all your failures
> protect you from your fears
>
> rub your head and stroke your hair
> hold you on your worst day
>
> and put them in my pockets
> when they start to get in your way

and when the balance shifts
as it always will do
these hands will pray that my mistakes
get the same Upper Hand from you

Seeds

within the bud
the unfolding
of the delicate Rose

within the acorn
the dream
of the mighty Oak grows

within the bean
the hope
of the twisted Vine

within the cone
the trunk
of the towering Pine

within the shell
the flight
of the Hummingbird

within her heart
the sweetest
Song ever heard

Metamorphosis

beauty
full wings
spread wide

floating
freedom
lonely

spectator
assumes
contentment

but butterfly
misses comfort
in the cocoon

the appeal
of flying
never was sky

she always
imagined
sharing the view

Dream Me Home

last night I dreamt of your kiss
we kissed each other
with abandon

as if no time had passed
as if nothing
had happened

in delight
in complete
comfort

and as truth dawned on us
and memories flooded in
we cried and cried

tears of release
tears of relief
home

Aging

the oranges, the browns, the reds
in the leaves
were always there
obscured by the green
of youth and activity

but at the first hint
of autumn's discomfort
the green is making its retreat

revealing the hidden beauty
that was patiently waiting
to take my breath away

Walk with Cardinal

to understand anything
you must go out
far enough
into nature

where the bird song
drowns out the city din

and then wait

until the bird song
drowns out the stories in your head

and then wait

until you are
the bird song

www.ingramcontent.com/pod-product-compliance
Lightning Source LLC
Chambersburg PA
CBHW021412290426
44108CB00010B/498